1/12

CR

FREEDOM AND THE FUTURE

BY JIM OLLHOFF

VISIT US AT
WWW.ABDOPUBLISHING.COM

Printed in the United States of America, North Mankato, Minnesota.
052011
092011

 PRINTED ON RECYCLED PAPER

Editor: John Hamilton
Graphic Design: Sue Hamilton
Cover Design: Neil Klinepier
Cover Photo: AP
Interior Photos and Illustrations: AP-pgs 6, 8, 9, 11, 13, 18, 19 (left), 22, 23, 24, 25, 26, 27, 28 & 29; Corbis-pgs 15, 16 & 17; Getty Images-pgs 7, 10, 12 & 19 (right); NASA-pg 20; RavenFire-pg 4, ThinkStock-pg 5; White House-pgs 14 & 21.

Library of Congress Cataloging-in-Publication Data

Ollhoff, Jim, 1959-
 Freedom and the future / Jim Ollhoff.
   p. cm. -- (Hispanic American history)
 Includes index.
 ISBN 978-1-61783-056-3
 1. Hispanic Americans--History--Juvenile literature. 2. United States--Civilization--Spanish influences--Juvenile literature. I. Title.
 E184.S75O45 2012
 973'.0468--dc23
                        2011018224

CONTENTS

HISPANICS IN AMERICA

The Hispanic population is a quickly growing minority in the United States. People usually identify themselves as Hispanic, or Latino, if they or their ancestors came from Mexico, the Caribbean islands, or from the Spanish-speaking countries of South and Central America. People of Hispanic descent may be of any skin color.

According to the 1970 census, there were 9.6 million Latinos in the United States. By 1980, the Latino population had grown to 14.6 million. By 1990, it had grown to 22.4 million. In 2000, the population was at 35.3 million, and in 2010 it was projected at 47.8 million. The United States Census Bureau believes the Latino population will grow by 10 to 15 million people every 10 years for the foreseeable future. Today, about 15 percent of the population of the United States identify themselves as Hispanic.

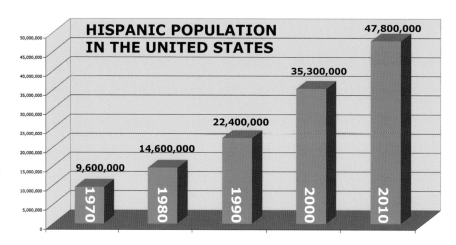

The U.S. Hispanic population has grown continually for many years.

HISPANIC POPULATION IN THE UNITED STATES

Year	Population
1970	9,600,000
1980	14,600,000
1990	22,400,000
2000	35,300,000
2010	47,800,000

People of Hispanic descent may be of any skin color.

Every state in America has Hispanic businesses, and the numbers are growing.

Most of the Hispanic population in the 1900s settled in Florida, Texas, New Mexico, Arizona, California, and Nevada. Many Latinos in the twenty-first century have also settled in Oregon, Idaho, Washington, Colorado, Wyoming, Utah, New York, Illinois, and along the East Coast of the United States. Some of the fastest growing places for Latinos are in the southeastern United States.

The most recent Hispanic population growth comes largely from Mexico. Most of the United States's Hispanic immigration, about 64 percent, is from Mexico. About nine percent of new Hispanic immigrants come from Puerto Rico.

The number of Hispanic business owners grows every year. Today, about two million Latinos own businesses. Far more run major businesses and corporations.

Hispanic culture has had a huge influence on the United States. Signs of Hispanic culture are everywhere. From architecture and art, to literature, language, food, and dress, Hispanic culture is seen in every city and state in the United States.

A woman holds her Certificate of Naturalization after being officially sworn in as an American citizen in Fort Lauderdale, Florida.

1950s & 1960s CIVIL RIGHTS IN AMERICA

World War II ended in 1945. The Nazis, led by Adolf Hitler, were defeated. Thousands of Hispanic-American citizens served their country by fighting for freedom. However, when the Hispanic soldiers came home, they found they had to fight for freedom again. This time, these Americans had to fight for their civil rights—to be treated like Americans.

In the 1960s and 1970s, Congress passed several laws that made it illegal to discriminate. It became illegal to not give services, such as education, to people who don't speak the English language. The Supreme Court ruled on several cases that made it easier on people who did not speak English.

The United States Declaration of Independence says that all people are created equal. In the 1950s, 1960s, and 1970s, African Americans, Asians, women, and Hispanics demanded to be treated equally. While racism, ignorance, and hatred are still with us today, the United States has made big strides in reducing racism's power.

Hispanic civil rights leader César Chávez (holding microphone) leads a rally of the United Farm Workers as they struggled for fair pay and better benefits from their employers.

MUSIC

Ritchie Valens

Sometimes it takes a single person to blaze a new trail that opens the door for others. One of the first Hispanic musicians to hit the mainstream was Ritchie Valens. This talented singer and musician was a Mexican American born in the United States in 1941. In 1958, he released his biggest hit, "La Bamba." It was based on a Mexican folk song. Tragically, Valens's career was cut short when he was killed in a plane crash in Iowa in 1959.

Gloria Estefan

Jennifer Lopez

Ricky Martin

Shakira

Ritchie Valens blazed a trail for other Hispanic artists to introduce their music styles to people in the United States. There are now hundreds of Latino artists who play all kinds of music. These include the peaceful pan flutes of the Andes, the uptempo calypso and reggae of the Caribbean islands, Latin jazz and pop, New York salsa, and Texas Tejano music. From the powerful voices of Gloria Estefan and Jennifer Lopez, to the passionate pop of Shakira and Ricky Martin, Hispanic music is here to stay.

TELEVISION

Lucille Ball and Desi Arnaz in an episode of *I Love Lucy.*

In 1961, the Spanish International Network became the first Spanish-language television network in the United States. Its programming helped to keep Hispanic language and culture alive for those living in the United States. Today, the network is known as Univision.

One of the first Hispanic actors with a regular role on a weekly television show was Desi Arnaz. He played the husband of Lucille Ball on the hit comedy series *I Love Lucy.* He not only played her husband, he actually was her husband in real life. Network executives were unsure at first if American audiences would be bothered by his Cuban accent. He was not only accepted, but became famous and well loved in his role. He died of lung cancer in 1986.

Some of the early Latino actors endured prejudice and racism, but fought through it. Because of them, today there are endless numbers of Hispanic actors and actresses on television.

Freddie Prinze of Chico and the Man

George Lopez of The George Lopez Show

Selma Hayek guest starred on 30 Rock

Eva Longoria of Desperate Housewives

Edward James Olmos of Miami Vice

13

A CIVIL RIGHTS HERO: CESAR CHAVEZ

The 1960s brought about much change in the United States. Blacks were demanding an end to injustice and separation. Women were demanding equal pay for equal work. College students and others protested the unpopular war in Vietnam. People spoke about the need for civil rights—the rights of every human to have equality and freedom from injustice. Martin Luther King Jr.

President Lyndon Johnson signs the Civil Rights Act of 1964. Martin Luther King Jr. stands behind him.

became the most famous civil rights hero. He worked tirelessly in the black community until he was killed by an assassin's bullet in 1968.

Hispanic people also had a civil rights hero. His name was César Chávez, and he worked faithfully for the Latino community until his death in 1993.

Chávez was born in Arizona in 1927. His family was desperately poor. They worked on a farm, tending crops. They lived with very little money, and they had to endure a lot of prejudice. Despite the challenges of poverty and prejudice, his family taught him the importance of education and hard work.

César Chávez was a farm worker until he took a job with a Latino civil rights group in 1952.

15

In the 1950s and 1960s, Hispanic farm workers, mostly of Mexican descent, worked on farms for long hours and terribly low wages. César Chávez helped to organize farm workers so they could demand better wages and working conditions.

Beginning in California, he organized farm workers into unions. When farm owners refused to give better wages, the unions went on strike, or refused to work. This meant that the farm produce was not getting picked when it was ripe, which was very costly to farm owners.

In 1965, César Chávez helped organize farm workers in a protest march to the California state capitol in Sacramento.

In 1965, Chávez organized a march to the California state capitol in Sacramento to protest the treatment of farm workers.

Like Martin Luther King Jr., Chávez advocated active non-violent protests. He organized marches, boycotts, and other protests to help those who were victims. He worked his whole life so that others would be treated with respect and dignity. César Chávez's birthday, March 31, is now recognized by California as a state holiday.

SPORTS

Roberto Clemente was inducted into the Baseball Hall of Fame in 1973.

One of the first Hispanic athletes to rise to national prominence was Roberto Clemente (1934-1972). He played Major League Baseball for the Pittsburgh Pirates starting in 1955. He was a fearsome outfielder because his speed and catching ability were matched by the laser-like accuracy of his throwing arm. He won the Gold Glove Award for outfield play 12 years in a row, and won 4 batting titles. In 1972, he was tragically killed in a plane crash while aiding earthquake victims in Nicaragua. He was the first Hispanic player inducted into the Baseball Hall of Fame.

Nancy Lopez

Oscar De La Hoya

Nancy Lopez (1957-) was one of the first Hispanic female professional golfers. Beginning her career in 1977, she won 48 Ladies Professional Golf Association tournaments.

Hispanic boxer **Oscar De La Hoya (1973-)** won the gold medal at the 1992 Olympic Games in Barcelona, Spain. In his famous career, he won 10 world titles in a variety of weight classes.

OTHER HISPANIC HEROES

Dr. Ellen Ochoa is a Hispanic astronaut for the National Aeronautics and Space Administration (NASA). She was born in California in 1958. She went to college in San Diego, and earned her doctorate degree in electrical engineering at Stanford University in California. She became an astronaut in 1991. Her first space mission was on the space shuttle *Discovery* in 1993, to study the sun's effect on Earth.

In 1994, she was the mission's payload commander. In 1999, she flew on *Discovery* to deliver supplies to the International Space Station. In 2002, she returned to the International Space Station to install equipment and bring supplies. She retired from spacecraft flights and in 2007 became deputy director of the Johnson Space Center in Houston, Texas.

Sonia Sotomayor is the first Hispanic United States Supreme Court justice. She was born in 1954 in New York City. Her parents were from Puerto Rico. She worked as a lawyer and as an assistant district attorney. She taught at law schools and worked for organizations that advocated for Latinos. She was nominated for the U.S. District Court in New York, and then later served on the U.S. Court of Appeals. In 2009, President Barack Obama nominated her for appointment to the United States Supreme Court.

Bill Richardson has served as a U.S. congressman, the U.S. ambassador to the United Nations, secretary of energy, and as governor of New Mexico.

Bill Richardson is an important Hispanic government official. He was born in California in 1947. His career in politics included being the governor of New Mexico from 2003 to 2011. He also was the United States ambassador to the United Nations, a United States Congressman representing New Mexico, and the secretary of energy in President Bill Clinton's administration. He ran for president in 2008, but lost the Democratic primary contest to President Barack Obama.

Oscar de la Renta stands with former First Lady Laura Bush.

Oscar de la Renta (1932-) is a successful Hispanic fashion designer based out of New York City. He was born in the Dominican Republic, but became an American citizen in 1971. He originally studied to become an artist. In 1961, he took his first job in fashion in Paris. His clothing styles became famous.

In 1963, he moved to the United States, where he became known for his suits and ball gowns. His gowns have been worn by several first ladies, including Nancy Reagan, Hillary Clinton, and Laura Bush. De la Renta won many fashion awards, including the Women's Wear Designer of the Year Award in 2000.

Illegal Mexican immigrants wait to cross the desert between Sasabe, Mexico, and Sasabe, Arizona. Immigrants often find work on farms, where conditions are poor, and they are not paid fairly.

THE PROBLEM OF ILLEGAL IMMIGRANTS

In order to live in the United States, a person must either be a citizen of this country or have the proper papers to be here legally. Visitors to the United States must have a passport, a document that allows them to come into the country, stay for a certain length of time, and then return home. Some people are citizens of another country—for example, Mexico—but they work in the United States. These people need a visa, which is a document or a stamp on their passport, which allows them to be in the United States for a particular purpose, like working at a job.

Passports and visas are expensive and take a long time to get. Some people enter the country illegally, without the proper documents. They might sneak across the border at night, then meet up with a contact who takes them somewhere to work. Illegal immigrants often work on farms, where they harvest vegetables or tend the crops.

Illegal immigration has been a complicated problem for many decades. Unable to find work at home, illegal immigrants often work for very little pay in the United States. This benefits the immigrants because they can work and earn some money, but it also cheats them out of an honest wage. Employers may give them only a fraction of the money that they would pay an American citizen. They know the illegal immigrants can't complain to the authorities for fear they would be expelled, or deported, from the United States. People in the United States have often overlooked this problem because the arrangement means that their food prices stay lower, since farm employers pay the workers so little.

However, early in the twenty-first century, some people began to blame illegal immigrants for an economic slowdown in the United States. They said illegal immigrants were stealing jobs from Americans. Advocates for the illegal immigrants said that the immigrants were filling jobs that American citizens didn't want. But critics's voices grew louder, and the federal government began building a fence along the Mexican border to stop people from sneaking across. Parts of the fence were completed, but other parts were abandoned because it was too expensive. The debate about illegal immigrants is complicated and emotional, and it is not likely to go away any time soon.

A U.S. Border Patrol agent drives along the U.S.-Mexico border in Jacumba, California, as men wait on the Mexican side for sunset to attempt an illegal crossing from Ejido Jacume, Mexico.

FREEDOM AND THE FUTURE

Today, nearly 48 million Latinos living in the United States bring richness to our national culture.

Hispanics come from Mexico, the Caribbean islands, and Central and South America. More than 20 different countries and territories are considered Hispanic, and they each have a flavor that is different than everyplace else.

The United States has always been a mix of many different cultures. We are all stronger and better when many cultures mesh.

We are always best when we work together and play together, and sit down together to talk when problems arise.

Hispanic culture brings a rainbow of richness to the United States. Many brave Hispanic pioneers have paved the way for their peers and other cultures in sports, music, government, and every other place in American society. These pioneers have taught us that, with hard work, we can do anything!

More than one million mostly Hispanic immigrants and their supporters took to the streets of Los Angeles, California, for an immigration rally in 2006.

GLOSSARY

BOYCOTT

A way of protesting unfair or bad business practices by having large numbers of people stop buying or using certain products or services. In 1965, grape pickers in Delano, California, wanted better pay for their hard work. They encouraged all Americans to stop buying grapes. This brought national attention to the area and grape purchases decreased. This caused the farm owners to lose a lot of money, and forced them to pay their workers better.

CARIBBEAN

The islands and area of the Caribbean Sea, roughly the area between Florida and South and Central America.

CENSUS

A government's records that show information about who lives in a country and where they live. Also, the process of collecting that information. In the United States, this happens once every 10 years.

CIVIL RIGHTS

The rights that individuals have, to not be harassed by the government or private organizations. These might include the right to vote, the right to a fair trial, and the right to equal treatment.

CULTURE

All the things that make up how we live, including food, music, language, architecture, dress, and customs.

Immigrant

A person who has entered a country intending to live there permanently.

Passport

An official document that allows for travel from a person's home country to another country.

Supreme Court

The United States Supreme Court is the highest court in the country. There are nine judges on the Supreme Court. They make sure local, state, and federal governments are following the rules spelled out in the United States Constitution. Our understanding of the Constitution evolves over time. It is up to the Supreme Court to decide how the Constitution is applied to today's society. When the Supreme Court rules on a case, other courts in the country must follow the decision in similar situations. In this way, the laws of the Constitution are applied equally to all Americans.

Union

Employees who have joined together to work as a group to establish pay and benefits with business owners.

Visa

A stamp or certificate issued to people entering another country so they can visit, travel, or work for a specific amount of time.

World War II

A conflict across the world, lasting from 1939-1945. The United States entered the war in December 1941.

INDEX